D1372477

"Those Are MY Private Parts" is a wonderful resource for parents and professionals alike. Written with preschoolers in mind, it offers an easy, non-threatening way for parents to begin the important early education of keeping their children safe from sexual abuse. While most developmentally appropriate for children ages 3 to 5 years old, the book will help open the door for continuing matter-of-fact discussions as children get older.

The author has found an engaging way to promote developmentally appropriate conversation with children regarding a crucial topic. Without making parents feel uncomfortable or inadequate, she helps convince parents of the importance of openly addressing this child safety issue, just as we would with other safety issues, such learning to cross the street, etc. She also provides a logical plan of action for kids to talk to trusted adults and to help them begin to learn to set appropriate boundaries.

I highly recommend the book for parents, preschool teachers, health care professionals, family therapists and anyone working with or providing care to young children, and in fact give copies of the book as "door prizes" when facilitating child sexual abuse prevention classes. Thank you Diane for providing a wonderful resource for what can be an uncomfortable topic!

Marcia Stanton, MSW
Child Abuse Prevention Coordinator
Phoenix Children's Hospital Phoenix, AZ

I received your book and have already had a chance to read it to one of my 4 year old clients. When I finished, he said, "Read it again". He loved saying, "Those are MY Private Parts," with me each time I read it. Also showed it to a colleague who wants to borrow it for a 3 year old client next week. It is an adorable book and well done. I am happy to have it because it seems there is little written for the little ones that they really understand. Congratulations on this great project! I will pass it on to more of my colleagues and they may want to order one. Thank you for being an important friend to children.

Dr. Karyl McBride, PhD, PC

"This is a vibrantly illustrated and creative approach to educating children about the right they have to protect their bodies, and the need to say NO! Those Are My Private Parts will likely unsettle people who are unaccustomed to speaking with their children about their intimate anatomy. It will probably shock people who cannot imagine a child having drawn the pictures in this book. All the more reason to clear that mental impediment, and get on with the vitally important work of teaching children about their bodies, and their rights. When we empower our children, we empower a future without child sexual abuse."

Carol A. Redding, CEO
Health Presentations
The ACE Study - www.acestudy.org

"The ACE Study reveals a powerful relationship between our emotional experiences as children and our physical and mental health as adults, as well as the major causes of adult mortality in the United States. It documents the conversion of traumatic emotional experiences in childhood into organic disease later in life. How does this happen, this reverse alchemy, turning the gold of a newborn infant into the lead of a depressed, diseased adult? The Study makes it clear that time does not heal some of the adverse experiences we found so common in the childhoods of a large population of middle-aged, middle class Americans. One does not 'just get over' some things, not even fifty years later."

Those are
MY
PRIVATE PARTS

Written by: Diane Hansen
Illustrations by: Charlotte Hansen

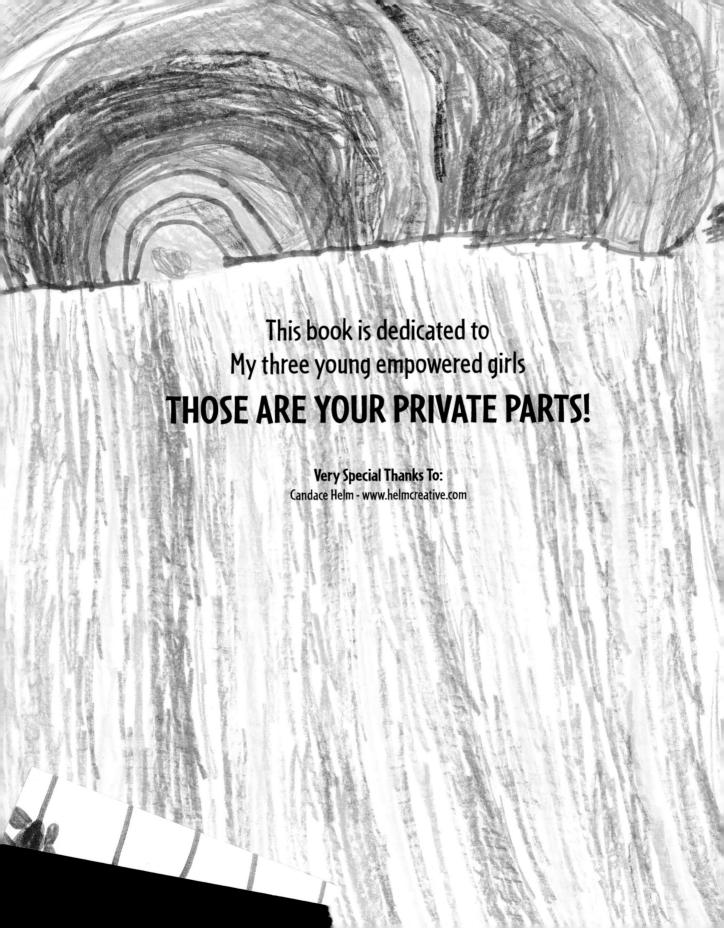

This book is dedicated to
My three young empowered girls

THOSE ARE YOUR PRIVATE PARTS!

Very Special Thanks To:
Candace Helm - www.helmcreative.com

Dear Concerned Adult,

Thank you for choosing to read "Those are MY Private Parts" to your children. This book is intended to help adults and children learn how to talk about what is okay and what is not okay when it comes to touching private parts of the body. Why is there a need for such a book? Unfortunately, perpetrators of sexual misconduct use trickery to get children to participate. Children may be told that they are "playing a game" or that they will be rewarded with candy or a treat if they participate. Afterwards, they are told "not to tell anyone" or something bad will happen. 1) Children do not know that the "game" of touching their private parts is wrong. 2) Children do not know that even if threatened not to tell, they still can tell a caring and safe adult. A caring and safe adult can help the child and stop these "games."

One of the goals of this book is to open healthy communication between children and adults so that children can come forward and talk about their feelings, experiences, questions, and concerns. This book encourages dialogue about personal matters and establishes you as a safe adult who the child can talk to.

We have found that education is the best prevention of inappropriate sexual behavior. However, if something does happen, early detection is important to stop the behavior, get the child to safety, and to seek medical help. Some warning signs may be: if you notice sudden changes in your child such as becoming quiet, sullen, or sad; having nightmares; being unusually anxious or fearful; avoiding social situations; afraid of being left alone with someone in particular; exhibiting irritability, angry outbursts, or aggressive behaviors towards others; or enacting sexual play between dolls or stuffed animals. If you notice your child is upset, ask if something happened and encourage him or her to talk with you.

If sexual misconduct does occur, children are not to be blamed for the event. Children tend to blame themselves and may think they are "bad" because of what happened. Perpetrators know this and may tell them "it is your fault" or "you deserve this." Safe and caring adults can reassure children that they were in a situation where someone tricked them and over-powered their right to say "no." Tricking people into doing things is wrong. But, what the child did was not their fault. Adults can offer praise and encouragement to let them know that they are loved and are indeed "good children."
Thank you for taking the time to read this book and to talk with your children.

With best regards,
Lori Katz, Ph.D., Clinical psychologist, Director of the Sexual Trauma Center
Department of Veterans Affairs, Long Beach Healthcare System, California, USA

This is where the learning starts
About boys and girls and private parts.
The front is different; the back the same.
And most of all, there is no private parts game.

THOSE ARE **MY** PRIVATE PARTS!

Private parts for boys
FRONT

BACK

Private parts for girls
FRONT

PENIS

Bottom,
Butt or
Rear
DO NOT
Get Near!

VAGINA

There are no touching or feeling games
Where private parts have different names.
Yours or mine, I do not share,
No one touches me down there.

THOSE ARE **MY** PRIVATE PARTS!

There is no private parts game to play.
It is wrong and not okay!
Not with my uncle, nephew, niece or dad,
I am strong and I WILL GET **MAD!**

THOSE ARE **MY** PRIVATE PARTS!

Aunts, cousins, step-fathers, step-brothers
Nannies, grannies, pa-pas or mothers.
Never will anyone make me play,
A private parts game in any way.

THOSE ARE **MY** PRIVATE PARTS!

Rubba-dub is for the tub

A babysitter, super-star, whoever they may be.

Will never, ever play a touching game with me.

I do not have to play.

"GET AWAY," I will say.

THOSE ARE **MY** PRIVATE PARTS!

Not the neighbor down the street,
Or anyone that I meet.
What about the kind neighbor next door?
My body is MINE forever more.

THOSE ARE **MY** PRIVATE PARTS!

My body belongs just to me.
The one and only me, you see.
It's my body from my head to my toe
"NO!" I can say, to anyone I know.

THOSE ARE MY PRIVATE PARTS!

I am young and have a big, loud voice.

It is MY body, it is MY choice.

I am strong and I am so brave.

I know the right way to behave.

THOSE ARE **MY** PRIVATE PARTS!

Bathroom words are potty, poop and pee.

I am big and I take care of me.

If I need help with these

I may say, "Help me please."

THOSE ARE MY PRIVATE PARTS!

I own my body. It is MINE!
Only for me, myself and I.
I will tell someone right away.
I own my body everyday.

THOSE ARE MY PRIVATE PARTS!

I will take a long and trusting look
at the person reading me this book.
This person will believe me.
With whatever it may be.

A tickle, rub or even a pat.
It is okay if I don't like that.

THOSE ARE **MY** PRIVATE PARTS!

Anyone that I love and trust,
LISTEN TO ME, IT IS A MUST!
You will never, ever touch or play
with my private parts in any way.

THOSE ARE MY PRIVATE PARTS!

Not for money, candy or a special trip,
THOSE ARE MY PRIVATE PARTS!
GET IT!

A NOTE TO PARENTS:

Your children may have many questions or none at all. It is important to talk and promote an open conversation. A child's body is developing and a part of development is sexuality. Children are aware of their sexual parts from a very early age. It is important we talk about our child's new discoveries with them. Spoken by convicted child molesters, "Parents are partly to blame if they don't tell their children about sex-I used it to my advantage by teaching the child myself." "Parents shouldn't be embarrassed to talk about things like this-its harder to abuse or trick a child who knows what you're up to." Parents and caregivers can initiate discussions about children's sexuality in many ways. While reading this book, stop and pause after each page and wait for a question from your child. The book is short, take your time. The book begins with an important message, "There is no private parts game." My 3 year old daughter asked, "What is a private parts game?" I simply replied, "There is no game where your vagina is in the game. If anyone wants to play a game where your vagina is touched or looked at, it is wrong and not okay. There is no game. That is your private part. No one else can touch it. It is special to only you. I love you and I want you to tell me if anyone tries to trick you, okay?" Let them know it is okay to tell you and you won't get mad. Tell your child you believe them and love them. Explain the illustrations for page 3 to your child. Identify your child's private parts with the correct names. Say vagina/penis out loud. Ask your child to say it. Go ahead; it's not a bad word. Tell your children you understand them and their body. Child molesters tell children, "I understand you and how your body feels and your parents don't."

Diane Hansen

....

"I read, Those are MY Private Parts to my 9 year old son. I have always spoken very openly with him. I thought it would be a little young for him. To my surprise he had several comments and questions after the 3rd page. He asked, 'Is it okay if I don't like being touched on my shoulders?' Thank you for reminding me to take every opportunity to open up communication with my son no matter how grown up I think he is."

June, Mother and Survivor

....

Copies of Those Are MY Private Parts can be purchaced from www.amazon.com
For Quantity Discounts please email: diane@thosearemyprivateprts.org

FACTS:

- 1 in 4 girls and 1 in 6 boys are sexually abused before their 18th birthday. (Simpson, C., Odor, R., & Masho, S. 2004 August. Childhood Sexual Assault Victimization in Virginia. Center for Injury & Violence Prevention. Virginia Department of Health.)

- An estimated 39 million survivors of sexual abuse exist in America. (Abel, G., Becker, J., Mittelman, M., Cunningham-Rathner, J., & Murphy, W. 1987. Self reported sex crimes on non-incarcerated paraphiliacs. Journal of Interpersonal Violence, 2(1), 3-25.

- Only 29% of parents ever mention or discuss sexual abuse with their children. That is, 71% of parents never talk about sexual abuse or sexual abuse prevention with their children. (Finkelhor, D. 1986 Sourcebook on Child Sexual Abuse; Sage p. 229.)

- More than half of all juvenile victims were younger than age 12. That is, 33% of ALL victims of sexual assault reported to law enforcement were ages 12 through 17. An astounding 34% were under the age of 12. (Snyder, H)

- The most disturbing fact is 14% of ALL victims or one in every seven victims of sexual assault reported to law enforcement agencies were UNDER AGE 6. (Snyder, H)

- The median age for reported sexual abuse is 9 years old. (Putnam, F. 2003. Ten-year researches update review: Child sexual abuse. Journal of the American Academy of Child and Adolescent Psychiatry, 42, 269-278.

- Only one in ten child victims reports the abuse. (Janssen, M. 1994. Incest, Exploitative Child Abuse; The Police Chief Magazine, 51, 46-7.)

- Most child victims NEVER REPORT the abuse. (Kilpatrick, D., Saunders, B., & Smith, D., 2003. Youth Victimization: Prevalence and Implications. U.S. Department of Justice, National Institute of Justice report.

- Children often fail to report because of the fear that disclosure will bring consequences even worse than being victimized again. Such as parents not believing, Daddy moving out and losing all financial support, tearing family apart, parents blaming child, parents thinking the child is at fault. (Berlinger, L. & Barbieri, M.K. 1984. The Testimony of the Child Victim of Sexual Assault. Journal of Social Issues, 40, p. 125–137.)

- 93% of all victims know their abusers. (Bureau of Justice Statistics, 2000, Sexual Assault on Young Children as Reported to Law Enforcement; US Department of Justice, Office of Justice.)

- Records indicate, in cases involving victims younger than 6, the perpetrators were strangers in only 3% of sexual assaults. Strangers committed the crimes against children, aged 6-11, in only 5% of the cases. (Snyder, H.)

- Nearly 5 of every 6 sexual assaults of young juveniles occurred in residence. (Snyder, H.)

- "As some researchers have begun to suspect, it may be the case that a growing number of stepfathers are really 'smart pedophiles', who marry divorced or single women with families as a way of getting close to children." (Crewdson, J. 1988. By Silence Betrayed: Sexual Abuse of Children in America. p. 31)

- It is estimated that children with disabilities are 4 to 10 times more vulnerable to sexual abuse than their non-disabled peers. (National Resource Center on Child Sexual Abuse, 1992.)

- Young victims may not recognize their victimization as sexual abuse possibly because the child is tricked by a game or the child's first sexual experience is manipulated by the perpetrator. (Gilbert, N. 1998. Teaching Children to Prevent Sexual Abuse. The Public Interest, 93, 3-15.)

- The FBI estimates that there is a sex offender living in every square mile of the United States. How well do you know your neighbor?

- Locate sex offenders http://www.meganslaw.ca.gov or http://www.mapsexoffenders.com

It is highly likely that you know a child who has been or is being sexually abuse. It is also likely that you know an abuser. The greatest risk to our children doesn't come form strangers but from family and friends.

WE ALL HAVE A RESPONSIBILITY TO PROTECT THE CHILDREN IN OUR LIVES.

DARKNESS 2 LIGHT

Dear Diane,

Thank you so much for your note. I love Charlotte's artwork!

It is only through the support of dedicated individuals like you that Darkness to Light is able to carry out its mission of reducing the incidents of child sexual abuse.

Your book, Those are My Private Parts, is a simple, age-appropriate work which gives children the "okay" to say "no" to adults. In a charming rhyming style, you give children the power and permission to "own" their bodies, which is critically important to developing their sense of self."

Darkness to Light firmly believes that it is adults' responsibility to keep kids safe from the horror of child sexual abuse, but your text empowers children in such a way that, hopefully, they are comfortable saying "no."

Thank you again for your work.

Very truly yours,
Anne Lee
President and CEO, Darkness to Light
www.darkness2light.org

"Those are MY Private Parts is a delightful and engaging contribution to helping parents educate children about the importance of learning to set boundaries and what that looks like."
Kathleen Brooks, Ph.D. • Host of Darkness to Light: Breaking the Conspiracy of Silence • www.ethicalife.com

Darkness to Light designed a revolutionary new sexual abuse prevention training program to educate adults to prevent, recognize and react responsibly to child sexual abuse, plus motivate them to courageous action. It is designed for organizations and corporations that serve children and youth. The three-hour program is interactive, providing a workbook, a video and the basic mechanics for dealing with this epidemic. It also incorporates the "7 Steps to Protecting Our Children," Darkness to Light's core, evidence-based educational tool for sexual abuse prevention. You will find that Stewards of Children is a comprehensive sexual abuse prevention program, incorporating all of the fundamentals necessary in creating organizational policies and procedures that keep children safe and for training staff and volunteers in child protection. This training can also serve as a great community outreach tool for parents and adults.

The program includes:
•Interactive workbook
•Video interviewing sexual abuse survivors and experts in the field
•Organizational policies and procedures manual
•Guidance in the identification of community resources for survivors, victims and their families
•On-going support through the Darkness to Light website and national helpline

This authorized Facilitator Workshop has been approved by the National Association of Social Workers as a provider of continuing education credit. This is the first national level approval for continuing education and attests to the integrity and quality of the curriculum.

To schedule a training program in Los Angeles or Orange Counties contact Diane Hansen at (310) 872-8206 or email diane@thosearemyprivateparts.org

TAALK - Talk About Abuse to Liberate Kids, Inc. - www.taalk.org

1 in 4 girls and 1 in 6 boys will be sexually abused before their 18ᵗʰ birthday [3, 4, 6, 7, 8, 11]

Although it's more comfortable to think of child sexual abuse in terms of "stranger danger," it's a fallacy that child molesters seek to exploit. In fact, child molesters appear most often in our inner circles.

30-40% of the time children are abused by a family member [2, 9, 12] Another 50% by someone the child knows and trusts [2, 5, 9]

Even if we can accept that abusers are people we know, we tend to hold on to the image of a middle-age man as the typical child molester. While men make-up the largest portion of the population of child molesters, we won't be in a position to truly protect children or effectively support survivors in our lives until we realize that child molesters can also be women and children.

40% of the time the abuser is an older or larger child [1, 9] 8% of abuse happens at the hands of the child's biological mother [10]

There are over 39 million survivors of child sexual abuse in America [1] and from them experts have documented the signs that appear in children after abuse as well as behavior patterns that appear **BEFORE** abuse occurs. So, with the right training, we can recognize when children are in danger and put boundaries in place to directly reduce the risk of abuse in our homes, neighborhoods and youth serving organizations.

Child sexual abuse is predictable and preventable and we <u>all</u> play a part in the solution.

Keeping the secret and living a lie isolates survivors and perpetuates self-sabotaging behaviors including trust and intimacy issues, bad boundaries, excessive drug and alcohol use, eating disorders, sexual promiscuity, and even crime. If you are a survivor you understand the impact it can have on your life – emotionally, physically and spiritually. Know that you are not alone, it was not your fault and you have the power to shift the blame back to where it belongs – on you abuser.

For more information, to find a support group or to schedule a prevention class please contact **Diane Cranley at 1-888-808-6558**

....

To Report Child Abuse: Call **911** or your local Child Protection Services agency or Call **1-800-4-A-CHILD** if you suspect abuse and need to talk it through.

To Learn Your Part in Preventing Abuse or Find Resources for Healing: Visit www.taalk.org or call **1-888-808-6558**

If You or Someone You Know Struggles with Inappropriate Feelings towards Children: Visit www.stopitnow.org or call **1-888-PREVENT**

....

1. Abel, G., Becker, J., Mittelman, M., Cunningham-Rathner, J., Rouleau, J., & Murphy, W. (1987). Self reported sex crimes on non-incarcerated paraphiliacs. Journal of Interpersonal Violence, 2(1), 3-25.

2. Abel, G. & Harlow, N. (2001) Stop child molestation book. Abel and Harlow.

3. Doll, L.S., Koenig, L.J., & Purcell, D.W. (2004) Child sexual abuse and adult sexual risk: Where are we now? In L.S. Doll, S.O. O'Leary, L.J. Koenig, & W. Pequegnat (Eds.) From Child sexual abuse to adult sexual risk (pp 3-10). Washington, DC: American Psychological Association.

4. Dube, S.R., Anda, R.F., Whitfield, C.L., Brown, D.W., Felitti, V.J., Doug, M., & Giles, W.H. (2005). Long-term consequences of childhood sexual abuse by gender of victim. American Journal of Preventive Medicine, 28, 430-438.

5. Elliott, M., Browne, K., & Kilcoyne, J. (1995). Child sexual abuse prevention: What offenders tell us. Child Abuse & Neglect, 5, 579-594.

6. Fergusson, D., Horwood, L., & Lynskey, M. (1997) Childhood sexual abuse, adolescent sexual behavior, and sexual revictimization. Child Abuse & Neglect, 21. 789-803.

7. Finkelhor, D., & Dziuba-Leatherman, J. (1994). Children as victims of violence: A national survey. Pediatrics, 94, 413-420.

8. Hooper, J. (1998). Child Abuse: Statistics, Research, Resources. Boston, MA: Boston University School of Medicine.

9. Kilpatrick, D., Saunders, B., & Smith, D. (2003). Youth victimization: Prevalence and implications. U.S. Department of Justice, National Institute of Justice report.

10. Sedlak, A.J., Mettenburg, J., Basena, M., Petta, I., McPherson, K., Greene, A., and Li, S. (2010). Fourth National Incidence Study of Child Abuse and Neglect (NIS-4): Report to Congress. Washington, DC: U.S. Department of Health and Human Services, Administration of Children and Families, 3-9.

11. Simpson, C., Odor, R., & Masho, S. (2004 August). Childhood Sexual Assault Victimization in Virginia. Center for Injury & Violence Prevention. Virginia Department of Health.

12. Snyder, H.N. (2000). Sexual assault of young children as reported to law enforcement: Victim, incident, and offender characteristics. National Center for Juvenile Justice, U.S. Department of Justice.

About Spanking...

Spanking–slapping/hitting of the buttocks–is physical violence. This fact alone is reason enough to make the spanking of children unacceptable by the same standards that protect adults, who are not as vulnerable. However, there is more to spanking than simple hitting. Spanking trespasses one of the body's most sensitive sexual areas–the genitals.

Furthermore, violent socialization of infants and children by 'spanking,' 'bopping,' 'switching,' 'licking,' 'whipping,' 'paddling,' 'popping,' 'whacking,' 'thumping,' etc. conditions children to accept and tolerate aggression and violence. This leaves the child prey to sexual abuse and incest. To address the inappropriateness of spanking children completely, we need to consider not only the issue of physical violence, but also the issue of sexual trespass.

It is a known fact that sex offenders target children who appear to have been victims before (quiet, withdrawn, compliant.) A previous victim of body boundary violations tend to be quiet, easy to manipulate and more likely to comply with a sex offender's demands.

The harm of spanking has been thoroughly explained and demonstrated over the past century in academic literature, scientific research, legal treatises, and recently in the popular media. We know that spanking is still considered the preferential form of child discipline as 22 states allow paddling with a wooden paddle in schools. Further evidence that spanking is a preferential form of child discipline is revealed in a random telephone survey done by Harvard Medical Center in 1997. 67% of parents surveyed stated they hit their child(ren) an average of once a week.

Some people believe spanking is justified or even commanded in the Bible–Proverbs. There is a distinction between the practice in King Solomon's day of beating adults on the back and modern practice of spanking/hitting children on the buttocks. The latter is not prescribed anywhere in the Bible.

Furthermore, the Old Testament contains passages that could be (and in some incidents have been) construed as divine endorsements of wife-beating, racial warfare, slavery, the stoning to death of rebellious children and other behaviors that are outrageous by today's standards.

Our laws and cultural values are unambiguous concerning adults who physically hit/slap or verbally threaten adults. It is recognized as criminal, and we hold the offenders accountable. Why then, when so much is at stake for society, do we accept the excuses of those who hit children? Why do we become interested in the needs of children only after they have been terribly victimized, or have become delinquents victimizing others?

The answer is: We cannot believe that hitting children is abuse until we can honestly acknowledge the mistreatment from our own childhood experiences and examine the shortcomings of our own parents. To the extent we feel compelled to defend our parents and guard their secrets, we will do the same for others. We will promote physical punishment as a 'standard' form of discipline or look the other way. By continually insisting that we 'turned out okay,' we are reassuring ourselves and diverting ourselves from deeply hidden unpleasant memories.

Recognition of the harm of spanking can only begin with an acknowledgment of the truth. It is futile to hope that denial, lies, evasions and excuses can somehow erase the memory and pain of past injuries.

Dorothy M. Neddermeyer, PhD, Author
"If I'd Only Known...Sexual Abuse in or out of the Family:
A Guide to Prevention, specializes in: Emotional healing and Physical/Sexual Abuse Recovery"
Order at www.drdorothy.net